Catiline
Voltaire
Translation by William F. Fleming

Start Publishing PD LLC
Copyright © 2024 by Start Publishing PD LLC

All rights reserved, including the right to reproduce this book or portions thereof in any form whatsoever.

Start Publishing PD is a registered trademark of Start Publishing PD LLC
Manufactured in the United States of America

Cover art: Shutterstock/Taisiya Kozorez

Cover design: Jennifer Do

10 9 8 7 6 5 4 3 2 1

ISBN 979-8-8809-0300-9

Contents

Dramatis Personæ. 4

Act I. 5

Act II. 13

Act III. 20

Act IV. 27

Act V. 36

Dramatis Personæ

Cicero
Septimus
Cæsar
Crassus
Catiline
Clodius
Aurelia
Cethegus
Cato
Lentulus-Sura
Lucullus
Conspirators
Martian
Lictors

In his preface to this play Voltaire says:

"The learned will not here meet with a faithful narrative of Catiline's conspiracy: a tragedy, they very well know, is not a history, but they will see a true picture of the manners of those times: all that Cicero, Catiline, Cato and Cæsar do in this piece is not true, but their genius and character are faithfully represented: if we do not there discover the eloquence of Cicero, we shall at least find displayed all that courage and virtue which he showed in the hour of danger. In Catiline is described that contrast of fierceness and dissimulation which formed his real character; Cæsar is represented as growing into power, factious, and brave; that Cæsar who was born at once to be the glory and the scourge of Rome."

ACT I.

SCENE I.

The Scene represents, on one side, the palace of Aurelia; on the other the temple of Tellus, where the senate assembled: At a distance, a gallery communicating to some private passages that lead from the palace of Aurelia to the vestibule of the temple.

[Soldiers at the bottom of the stage.] Yes, thou proud talker, thou vile instrument Of a deluded people, soon thy power Shall be no more; and thou whose savage virtue, Inflexibly severe, destroys the nation It means to save, imperious Cato, know Thy doom is passed, thou and the tyrant senate Must fall together; they who keep the world In bondage shall themselves be slaves; their chains Are forged already, and usurping Pompey Shall pay for dear bought honors with his blood. Cæsar, his haughty rival, shall oppose him, His equal Cæsar: he who, like myself, Was ever factious, shall assist my cause; The snare is laid, and Cæsar shall prepare The throne for Catiline; I'll make them all Subservient to my purpose: Cicero's self, The man whom most I hate, shall be my friend: My wife too may be useful, and may prove A step to greatness: fathers, husbands, all Those empty names mistaken mortals call Most sacred, hence, I give you to the winds: Ambition, I am thine.

SCENE II.

Catiline, Cethegus.

Catiline: Well, my Cethegus, Whilst Rome and our designs are hid in night, Say, hast thou called together our brave chiefs?

Cethegus: Even here, my lord, beneath this portico, Safe from the consul's prying eyes, and near That impious scene where our proud tyrants sit, Thy friends shall meet—already they have signed The solemn compact, and are sworn to serve thee. But how stands Cæsar, will he second us?

Catiline: He is a turbulent unruly spirit, And acts but for himself.

Cethegus: And yet without him We never shall succeed.

Catiline: I've laid a snare He cannot escape: my soldiers, in his name, Shall seize Præneste—he's been long suspected. This will confirm his guilt—the furious consul Shall soon accuse him to the senate—Cæsar Will hazard all to satiate his revenge. I'll rouse this sleeping lion from his den, And make him roar for me.

Cethegus: But Nonnius still Rules in Præneste; he's a friend to Rome. In vain already thou hast tried to tempt His stubborn virtue—what must be his fate?

Catiline: Thou knowest I love his daughter, though I hate Her surly father: long he strove in vain To thwart our mutual passion, and prevent Our private marriage, which at last the churl Unwillingly consented to: he feared To incur his angry party's high displeasure And the proud consul's—but I've made his pride Subservient to our purpose—he is bound By solemn oaths to keep our marriage still A secret: Sura only and Cethegus Are privy to it: this perhaps may serve More purposes than one: Aurelia's palace Conducts us to the temple; there I've placed My instruments of ruin, arms, and firebrands, To execute our great design: thy zeal To friendship much I owe, but more to love. Beneath the senate's sacred vault, beneath The roof of Nonnius will we sacrifice These tyrants—you, my friends, must to Præneste; You to the capitol; remember whom You serve, the oath that binds you, and the cause You are engaged in—thou, my loved Cethegus, Must watch o'er all, and guide the great machine.

SCENE III.

Aurelia, Catiline.

Aurelia: O Catiline, my lord, my husband, ease My troubled heart, remove my doubts, my fears, My horror, my despair—alas! what means This dreadful preparation?—every step I tread alarms me; why these soldiers, why With arms and torches is my palace filled? The days of Marius and of Sulla sure Are now returned, and discord reigns amongst us: Explain, my lord, this dreadful mystery: Do not turn from me—by the sacred tie That joins our hearts, by the dear babe thou lovest, I talk not to thee of its mother's danger, For thee alone I tremble: pity me, Pity a wretched wife, and tell me all.

Catiline: Know then, my life, my fortune, and my fame, Thy safety, and my own, the common cause, Demand a conduct which thy fears condemn: But if thou lovest me, let whate'er thou seest Be buried in thy breast: I mean to save

Rome's better part; the senate and the people Are disunited—danger threats the state On every side; I've taken the best means To make all well again.

Aurelia: I hope thou hast; But can we hide our hearts from those we love? Canst thou deceive me? yet what thou hast said Doubles my fears. Alas! thy looks are wild, And full of horror. What will Nonnius say When he shall see these dreadful preparations? The voice of nature, and the tender names Of father and brother oft have passed Unheard and unregarded when the cause Of Rome required it—well thou knowest our marriage Gave much offence, and when my angry father Returning, shall behold these sad effects Of our unhappy union, what, my lord, Must I expect? O why wilt thou abuse The power which love has given thee o'er a heart Devoted to thy service?—thou hast gained A party, but consider well my father, Cato, and Cicero, and Rome, and heaven, Are all thy foes: Nonnius perhaps may come This very day on purpose to destroy thee.

Catiline: Be not afraid, I know he cannot.

Aurelia: How?

Catiline: Whene'er he comes he must approve our purpose: I am not left at liberty to tell thee What we design, suffice it that his interest And mine are one: I know when he shall find The fair result, he then will join with me To pull down the proud tyrants he obeys: Trust me, Aurelia, what I do shall prove The fertile spring of everlasting glory And honor to you both—

Aurelia: Alas! the honor I fear is doubtful, and the danger certain: What seekest thou? wherefore wouldst thou urge thy fate? Is it not enough to rank among the first Of human kind, and rule the subject world? Why wouldst thou mount the giddy heights of power, And court destruction? my foreboding heart Already sees, and trembles at thy danger. Are these the promised joys of flattering love? The peace I hoped for? I have lost it now For ever: O, my lord, when last these eyes Were in a short and broken slumber closed, Methought I saw in flames imperial Rome; Saw murders, deaths, and rivers stained with blood, My father massacred in open senate, And thee, my Catiline, amidst a band Of vile assassins, breathing forth thy soul In dreadful agonies: I rose, and fled From these sad images to find my lord, My guardian, my protector—thou art here, And I, alas! am but the more unhappy.

Catiline: Away—thy omens fright not Catiline; Complain not, but be resolute: I want Thy courage, not thy tears, when I am serving Thee and my country.

Aurelia: Is it thus thou meanst To serve her? O, my lord, I know not what Thy purpose is, but were it fair and just Perhaps I might long since have been consulted; Our mutual interest claimed it from a husband: If thou dissemblest with me, I have cause To doubt, and to be wretched—Cicero Has long suspected thee, and Rome thou knowest Adores him.

Catiline: Whom? my hated rival?

SCENE IV.

Catiline, Aurelia, Martian.

One of the Conspirators.

Martian: Sir, The consul comes this way—by his command The senate meet; he wishes first to see And speak with you.

Aurelia: I tremble at his name.

Catiline: Why tremble at the name of Cicero? Let Nonnius fear and reverence him, disgrace His rank and character by mean submission; I pity the weak senator, but hoped To find in thee a noble soul: not thus, Remember, acted thy brave ancestors: Gods! that a woman, and a Roman, sprung From Nero's blood, should thus be void of pride Or of ambition! noble minds are ne'er Without them.

Aurelia: Mine perhaps thou thinkest is mean And timid; cruelty alone with thee Is courage; thy reproach is most unkind; But know me better; know that this fond wife, Whom thou contemnest, who has not power to change Or soften thee, has more of Roman in her Than thou canst boast; and, coward as she is, Can teach thee how to die.

Catiline: How many cares At once surround me!—Cicero comes but him I fear not: this Aurelia.—

SCENE V.

Cicero, Catiline, Chief of the Lictors.

Cicero: [To the Chief Lictor.] Do as I Command you—I'll try if I can sound This faithless heart; leave me alone with him: Sometimes a villain may be wrought by fear To better counsel, and renounce his purpose. Who's there? the proud plebeian, chosen by Rome To be her master? [Turns to Cataline.] Ere the senate meet, Catiline, I come for the last time to hold The friendly torch, and save thy wandering steps From the dread precipice of guilt and ruin.

Catiline: Who, thou?

Cicero: Yes, I.

Catiline: And is it thus thy hate Pursues me?

Cicero: Call it pity—but observe me. The capitol is weary of thy plaints, Thy factious cries, and bold impertinence; Rome, and the senate have, it seems, debased The consul's dignity by choosing me: Thy pride we know expected it, but how Hadst thou deserved it? was it by the name, Or family, thy valor, or the pride Of a loose prodigal in shows and feasts And idle pomp; could these entitle thee To such exalted honors? couldst thou hope To be the great dispenser of the laws, To guide the mistress of the world who rules O'er prostrate kings? had Catiline been what He ought to be, I might perhaps to him Have yielded the contested palm.—Hereafter Thou mayest support the state, but to be consul 'Tis fit thou first shouldst be—a citizen. Thinkest thou by vile reflections on my birth, My fortune, and my fame, to taint my honor, Or weaken the firm basis of my power? In our corrupted days it is not name, Or family, that Rome has need of: no: 'Tis virtue; and the pride of Cicero Hath ever been, that he should nothing owe To his forefathers—my nobility Springs from myself, and thine may end in thee.

Catiline: It ill becomes a temporary power, Like thine, to boast of its authority.

Cicero: Had Cicero used that power as thou deservest, Thou wouldst not have been here to question it: Thou who hast stained our altars with pollution And sacrilegious rage, thy days are numbered But by thy crimes: thy merit is to dare, To strike at all, dissemble, and betray: Thou hast abused the precious gifts that heaven Bestowed on thee for other purposes: Sense, beauty, courage, and heroic warmth, All the fair ornaments of human nature, In thee are but the instruments of ill. My voice, which still is raised to scourge the wicked, And plead for the oppressed, hath spared thee yet; Nor with the odious Verres ranked the name Of Catiline: but long impunity Hath made thee shameless, and insensible Of all reproof—thou hast betrayed the state: At Rome, and in Etruria all is discord, And foul confusion; Umbria is revolted; Præneste staggers in her faith; the soldiers Of barbarous Sulla, drenched in blood, come forth From their dark caves prepared for slaughter, armed By cruel Mallius; all are leagued with thee; Thy partisans declared, or secret friends, All are united in one guilty bond, And sworn to the destruction of their country: I know thee for their chief, for I have eyes On every side, and hands too, thou shalt find, That, spite of thee, shall vindicate the cause Of injured Rome; thy guilty friends shall feel My justice too: thou hast beheld me long But as thy rival, now behold thy judge, And thy accuser, who will force thee soon To answer for thy actions by those laws Which thou so oft hast trampled on unpunished, Those laws which thou contemnest, and I revenge.

Catiline: I've told you, sir, already, that your office But ill excuses this indecent freedom: But for that country's sake, whom both are bound To serve, I pardon your unjust suspicions; Nay, I do more, I honor your warm zeal; Blind though it be, in such a cause 'tis just: But do not thus reproach me for past errors, For the wild follies of impetuous youth, That soon are o'er; your senate is to blame, I followed their example; pomp and pride, Excess and luxury, the fruits of conquest, Are the time's vices, not the native bent Of Catiline's heart: I served the commonweal In Asia as a soldier, as a judge In Africa: spite of our domestic feuds, Did I not make the name of Rome revered Among the nations? I who have defended Shall ne'er betray her.

Cicero: Sulla too and Marius Both served their country well, and then destroyed her. Tyrants have all some specious show of virtue, And ere they break their country's laws support them.

Catiline: If you suspect each brave and gallant soldier, Let Cæsar, Pompey, Crassus be accused: Why fix on me amongst so many? why Am I the only object of your fears? Have I deserved it?

Cicero: That you best can tell. But wherefore deign I thus to answer you?

Catiline: The more I plead in my defence, the more Will Cicero condemn me: if as friend Thou talkest to me, thou but deceivest thyself, I am thy foe; if as a citizen, So too is Catiline; if as a consul, A consul's not a master, he presides But in the senate, I defy him there.

Cicero: Thou durst not; for I there can punish guilt: If thou art innocent, I will protect thee; If not, I charge thee, be not seen in Rome.

Catiline: This is too much: I will no longer bear Thy insults, though I scorn thy vague suspicions: Yet know I think the worst affront that thou Couldst put on Catiline, would be to protect him.

Cicero: [Alone.] Insolent traitor! means he thus to prove His innocence by false affected pride? Perfidious wretch, I'm not to be deceived, Nor shalt thou thus escape the watchful eye Of vengeance.

SCENE VI.

Cicero, Cato.

Cicero: Well, my friend, hast thou prepared For Rome's defence?

Cato: Your orders are obeyed; I have disposed the chiefs, and all are ready To march as you direct them; but I fear The people, nay the senate.

Cicero: Ha! the senate?

Cato: Ay—they are swollen with pride—and foul division Will soon enslave them.

Cicero: Much indeed I fear Our vices will avenge the conquered world; Our liberty and virtue are no more; But Rome may still have hope whilst Cato lives.

Cato: Alas! who serves his country often serves A most ungrateful mistress—even thy merit Offends the senate; with a jealous eye It views thy greatness.

Cicero: Cato's approbation Is recompense enough; thy honest praise Will more than balance their ingratitude; On that and on posterity alone I shall rely; let us perform our duty, And leave the rest to heaven.

Cato: How shall we stem The torrent of corruption? when I see, Even in this sacred temple, raised to virtue, Infamous treason rise with shameless front: Can we suppose that Manlius, that proud rebel, Would dare advance his standard, and blow up The flames of civil war, if greater powers Did not support him, if some secret foe Abetted not their vile conspiracy? The leaders of the senate may betray us; From Sulla's ashes may new tyrants rise: My just suspicions light on Cæsar.

Cicero: Mine On Catiline; perfidious, sordid, rash, And bold; he loves rebellion, and delights In novelty; more dangerous than Cæsar; I know him well; even now I parted from him: What passed between us but confirms me more In my suspicions; on his face I read Rage and resentment, the determined pride Of his fierce spirit, that no longer deigned To hide its purpose, but stood forth, and owned Its enmity to Rome.—I must discover His bold compeers, perhaps I may prevent His future crimes, and save my falling country.

Cato: Catiline has friends, and much I fear the power Of these united tyrants may prove fatal: Our forces are in Asia, and at Rome We are corrupted; but one upright man May save the state.

Cicero: If we unite, our country Has naught to fear—in factions discord soon Dissolves the tie: Cæsar perhaps may join them; But, if I know him right, his noble soul Will never stoop to serve a worthless tyrant; He loves his country still, and hates a master; Though soon the time will come when he shall strive To be one; both are eager for applause, And both ambitious: both are raised too high To meet in friendship long; by their division Rome may be saved; let us not tamely wait To see our country's ruin, or behold In shameful chains the masters of mankind.

ACT II.

SCENE I.

Catiline, Cethegus.

Cethegus: At length the torch is lit to set on fire Rome and the subject world; our army's nigh, And all is ready for the great event. Knowest thou meantime, my friend, what passes here?

Catiline: I know the consul's prudence, so he calls His cowardice, which deeply ruminates On future ills: like an unskilful pilot He sets up every sail for every wind, But knows not or which way the tempest comes, Or whither it may drive him—for the senate, I fear it not; that many-headed monster, So proud of conquest and nobility, Looks with an evil eye on Cicero; I know it hates him, so does Cæsar; Crassus Would gladly yield him up a sacrifice To our resentment; on their jealousy Depend my hopes—he's like a dying man, With feeble arm he struggles for a while, But soon shall sink beneath us and expire.

Cethegus: Envy I know attacks him, but his tongue Can soften all; he leads the captive senate.

Catiline: I brave him everywhere; despise his clamors, And smile at his resentment: let him rail To his last hour, and triumph in the shouts Of his admirers, I have other cares That sit more heavy on me.

Cethegus: What should stop Thy rapid progress in the paths of glory And happiness? Canst thou have aught to fear?

Catiline: My numerous foes I heed not, 'tis my friends I have most cause to dread; the jealousy Of Lentulus, the aspiring soul of Cæsar, And, above all, my wife.

Cethegus: Shall Catiline Be frightened at a woman's tears?—for shame, Leave her to indulge her visionary fears: I thought thou lovest her as a master should, And madest her but the servile instrument Of thy ambition.

Catiline: 'Tis a dangerous one: Rome and her child divide with me her love. Curse on the name of Rome, that even beneath The roof of Catiline those should dwell who love Their country! But before the important hour That must decide our fate, she shall be moved, She and her son—be that thy care, Cethegus: Our wives and children must not trouble us In those distressful moments—but for Cæsar—

Cethegus: What's to be done? if he refuse to join Our cause, shall we proscribe him; shall the names Of Cicero and of Cæsar be united?

Catiline: Let me consider—to cut Cæsar off— That were a dreadful sacrifice; methinks I cannot but admire him, and revere In him the honor of the Roman name: But where is Lentulus?

Cethegus: O fear not him; His pride we know will prompt him to believe That thou with him wilt share the sovereign power.

Catiline: Let him believe it still! the credulous fool! Thou seest, Cethegus, with what sublety I'm forced to manage these imperious spirits; Their rage, resentment, pride and jealousy: Knowest thou he dares even to be Cæsar's rival? To keep my friends within the pale of prudence Will cost me much more trouble than the ruin Of Cicero and Rome—to guide a party Is of all tasks the hardest.—

Cethegus: Lentulus Is here, my lord.

SCENE II.

Catiline, Cethegus, Lentulus-Sura.

Sura: In spite of my remonstrance You will rely on Cæsar, and confide In him alone; Præneste's in his power. And I must yield to him; but know I scorn it, The blood of Scipio was not made to yield.

Catiline: I've joined with Cæsar, but depend not on him; He may support our cause, or he may hurt it; I use his name, but 'tis for your advantage.

Sura: And what is there in Cæsar's name superior To yours or mine? why must we meanly court His favor? but because he's Pompey's rival Rome makes a God of him.—I am thy friend; Sura and Catiline may defy them all, And without Cæsar make the world their own.

Catiline: We may—thy conduct and approved valor Have ever been my best and surest hope; But Cæsar is beloved, respected, feared; The senate and the people all admire And court him; statesman, general, magistrate; In peace revered, and terrible in war; A thousand ways he charms the multitude; In short he will be necessary.—

Sura: Say Destructive rather—if to-day he shines Our equal, by to-morrow he will prove Our rival, and ere long perhaps our master; Trust me, I know him well, and therefore think Our party has not a more dangerous foe: Perhaps his haughty soul may yield to thee, But play the tyrant o'er the rest; for me, I cannot, will not, brook it—I've devoted My honor and my fortunes to thy service; But I renounce my plighted faith, renounce Thee and thy cause, if Cæsar is preferred.

Catiline: And so thou shalt—I'd sacrifice my life Rather than e'er permit a haughty rival To soar above us—Cæsar is our tool, Our instrument; to-day I flatter him, To-morrow can bring down his pride, perhaps Do more—thou knowest our mutual happiness And interest are my first and dearest care. [To Cethegus.] Away, and let Aurelia be prepared: Go; or her fond intruding love may ruin Our deep laid schemes, and mar the great design: Return some private way and meet me here, I wait for Cæsar.

Sura: Nothing's to be done. I find, without him—but I'll wait the event.

Catiline: Farewell: remember I rely on thee More than on Cæsar.—

Cethegus: I shall execute Your high command, and gather all our friends Before the standard of great Catiline.

SCENE III.

Catiline, Cæsar.

Catiline: Hail, godlike Cæsar, thou whom from the days Of Sulla I have ranked amongst my best And dearest friends, whose fortunes I foretold: Born as thou art to be the first of Romans, How suits it with thy pride to be the slave Of a plebeian, who forever thwarts And braves thee to thy face? I know thou hatest him; Thy piercing eye observes impatient Rome Contending for her freedom, will not Cæsar Assist his country to shake off her chains? The cause is noble, and the fate of millions Depends on this important crisis; thou Wilt join us—lookest thou not with jealous eye On Pompey still? dost thou not still abhor The surly Cato? canst thou serve the gods With half thy wonted zeal when the proud consul Presides at the altar? will thy noble spirit Bear these imperious rulers; soft Lucullus, Sunk in the arms of luxury and sloth; The greedy Crassus, grasping his large heaps Of ill-got wealth, enough to purchase Rome And all her venal sons? on every side Or faction or corruption reigns; the world Calls out on Cæsar; wilt thou hear her voice? Wilt thou redress and save thy falling country? Will Cæsar listen to his friend?

Cæsar: He will; And if the senate do thee wrong, step forth To plead thy cause; I never will betray thee; But ask no more.

Catiline: Are these the utmost bounds Of Cæsar's friendship, but to talk for him?

Cæsar: I've weighed the projects, and shall not oppose them; I may approve, but would not execute.

Catiline: I understand you, you are on that side Which fortune favors, and would stand aloof To mark the progress of our civil wars, And raise your fortunes on the common ruin.

Cæsar: No—I have nobler views; my hate of Cato, My jealousy of Pompey, the renown Of Cicero, conspire to make me wish I might surpass them all; fair glory calls, The banks of Seine, the Tagus, and the Rhine; I pant for honor, and for victory.

Catiline: If conquest is thy aim, begin with Rome; To-morrow we may reign the masters of her.

Cæsar: The enterprise is great, perhaps too bold; But, to be open with thee, though 'tis worthy Of Catiline, it suits not Cæsar.

Catiline: How!

Cæsar: I do not choose to serve.

Catiline: To share with Cæsar Were no dishonor to the most ambitious.

Cæsar: But power supreme is not to be divided: I'll not be dragged at Catiline's chariot wheels To grace his triumph: as a friend I love thee; But know that friend shall never be—my master: Even Pompey shall not—Sulla, whom thy valor Hath nobly followed in the race of glory, Whose courage I admire, whose lawless rage I ever shall abhor, enslaved proud Rome: But he deserved the glorious prize, subdued The Hellespont, and made Euphrates tremble: Asia was conquered: Mithridates owned His martial genius—but what noble deeds Hast thou to boast? what kings hast thou subdued? What seas has Catiline passed, what lands explored? Thou hast the seeds of greatness in thy nature; But to enslave thy country is above Thy present powers, above the powers of Cæsar: We have not strength, authority or name For such an enterprise. Rome soon must fall: But ere I will attempt to be her master, I will extend her empire and her glory; And if I forge my country's chains, at least Will cover them with laurels.

Catiline: Mine, perhaps, Is, after all, the shortest path to glory: How did your boasted Sulla rise to empire? He had an army, so has Catiline; Raised by myself alone, and not, like his, The gift of fortune; he observed with care The favorable hour, and well improved it: I have done more; have made the times and seasons Subservient to me. Sulla was a king. Wouldst thou be one? wilt thou be Cicero's slave, Or rule with Catiline?

Cæsar: Neither. To be free, For I no longer will dissemble with you, I esteem Cicero; but love him not, Nor fear him: though I love, I dread not thee. Divide the senate if thou canst, pull down The proud oppressors; thou hast my consent; But hope no more, nor dare to think that Cæsar Will ever be thy slave: I'll keep thy secret, And be thy friend or foe, as thou deservest it.

SCENE IV.

Catiline: If he supports us not, even let him fall The victim of his folly: Sulla knew And would have cut him off, but Sulla dared not: I know he is my secret enemy, As such I shall beware of him.

SCENE V.

Catiline, Cethegus, Lentulus-Sura.

Sura: What says The mighty Cæsar? is he friend or foe?

Catiline: His barren friendship only offers me A feeble aid; but we can do without him: Perhaps he may repent it; and meantime We've better pillars to support the fabric. Behold, the heroes come.

SCENE VI.

Catiline, the Conspirators.

Catiline: Hail, bold Statilius, Valiant Autronius, noble Piso, hail, Vargontes, and the rest of my brave friends, The first of men, the conquerors of kings, The great avengers of a world oppressed, This seat of empire soon shall be your own: The vanquished nations, which your valor gained, Were ravished from you by usurping tyrants; For the proud senate still your blood hath flowed; For them Tigranes, Mithridates fell; For them alone; and all your poor reward Was but to stand at distance, and adore Your haughty masters; but at length the hour Of vengeance is approaching: be prepared For no inglorious enterprise: I know Your souls would scorn a victory cheaply bought; But I will bring you noble conquests, full Of danger and of glory: seize, my friends, The golden opportunity: already I see your foes expiring at your feet. Rush on your prey, burn, plunder, and destroy; But, above all, let union guide your counsels: Even now Præneste falls: the brave remains Of Sulla's scattered forces march towards us: I shall command them, and Rome must be yours Petreius vanquished, I shall clear my way Even to the capitol: then you, my friends, Shall rise to empire, to a throne disgraced By worthless Romans, and by you restored To its true lustre: Curius and his band Will open me the gates; but tell me, friend, The gladiatorian cohorts, where are they? Will those brave veterans join our cause?

Lentulus-Sura: They will: Myself shall lead them in the dead of night, And arm them in this secret place.

Catiline: Mount Cælius— Is that secured?

Statilius: I've bribed the sentinels, And all is safe.

Catiline: You to mount Aventine Repair, and soon as Mallius shall display His colors, light your torches, spread destruction On every side; let the proscribed perish. Let Cicero—ye have sworn it—be my first My darling victim: Cæsar too must die, And Cato; these removed, the senate soon Will tremble and obey: already fortune Declares for us, and blinds them to their ruin: Within their walls, and almost in their sight We lay the snares of death, and mark them out For sacrifice: remember not to take up arms Before the appointed time: we must surprise Ere we destroy: let Cicero and Rome Perish together, and the lightning blast Before the thunder's threatening voice alarms them. Call not this deed a foul conspiracy; 'Tis a just war declared against the foes Of Rome and all mankind; reclaim your rights, The empire of the world, which base usurpers Had ravished from you. [To Cethegus and Lentulus-Sura.] Haste, ye gallant leaders, Haste to the senate; see your victims there: Hear your proud consul roar; 'tis the last time That he shall triumph there—now, worthy Romans, Swear by this sword, that with the blood of tyrants Shall soon be stained, to perish, or to conquer, With Catiline.

Martian: By thee and by this sword We swear with thee to perish or to conquer.

Another Conspirator: Perish the senate! perish all who serve, All who defend them! if there be amongst us A traitor, let him die.

Catiline: Away, this night Will finish all, and Rome shall be our own.

ACT III.

SCENE I.

catiline, cethegus, martian, septimus. **Catiline**: Are all things ready? do our troops advance?

Martian: Even so, my lord; the faithful Mallius comes Prepared to circle these devoted walls; Our friends impatient brook not dull delay, But urge each other to the bloody scene; We wait but thy command; appoint the hour When Rome must fall.

Catiline: Soon as I quit the senate Begin the sacrifice: let this great day Be sacred to destruction: but meantime Take special care the consul's busy friends Do not observe our motions.

Cethegus: Were it not Most prudent to destroy him in the senate? He has alarmed the people, and foresees Our every action.

Catiline: Knows he the revolt Of Mallius? knows he Catiline's deep designs? Knows he an army is approaching for me? Fear not, my friends, ours is no common cause, 'Tis fit the means should be proportioned to it: When vulgar mortals, grovelling and obscure, Form ill-digested schemes, and idle plans Of future greatness, if one slender wheel Is broke, it overthrows the whole machine: But souls like ours, a firm and chosen band, Plans deeply laid, the conquerors of kings, The sons of Mars, united to support And raise each other, these must be superior To Cicero's art, or Cicero's vigilance: We've naught to fear.

Cethegus: But is Præneste ours In Cæsar's name?

Catiline: Ay; that was my first stroke Of policy: the unsuspecting senate Will be deceived: I've whispered it abroad, That Nonnius hath conspired against the state, And half our credulous fools believe the tale. Ere he can clear his innocence, my army Will be in Rome, and all secured: away, Remove Aurelia: let no little cares Intrude to stop or hurt the great design.

SCENE II.

Aurelia, Catiline, Cethegus, etc.

Aurelia: [A letter in her hand.] There, Catiline, read Aurelia's fate and thine, Thy crime and thy just sentence.

Catiline: What rash hand— Ha! 'tis thy father's.

Aurelia: Read it.

Catiline: [Reads the letter.] "Death too long Hath spared me, and the child I loved too well Must finish my sad days: at length I suffer For my own follies, and that hapless marriage Which I consented to; I know the plots Of thy vile husband: Cæsar has betrayed us, And would have seized Præneste: thou partakest The treason: but repent, or perish with them." But how could Nonnius e'er discover that Which even the consul knows not?

Cethegus: This may prove Our ruin.

Catiline: [To Cethegus.] It may turn to our advantage. Aurelia, I must tell thee all: this day The world is armed in Catiline's defence: Say, in the hour of danger wilt thou serve A father or a husband?

Aurelia: To be silent, And trouble thee no more, were the commands Which Catiline laid on his neglected wife, Spite of her fond entreaties, prayers, and tears: What hast thou further to desire?

Catiline: Away: This moment, send that letter to the consul; I have my reasons; I would have him know, That Cæsar is as much to be suspected As I am: he's accused, and Catiline not So much as named: it is as I could wish. Take with thee our loved infant, and return not To bleeding Rome, till I am master there: Then thou shalt reign with me: our marriage yet Is kept a secret: I'll not have it known, 'Till at the head of our victorious army I shall proclaim it loud to Italy, And to the world: then shall thy haughty father, As our first subject, humbly bend before thee, And sue to be forgiven: begone, Aurelia, And leave me to my fate. I would not wish Thou shouldst partake my dangers or my cares: This night prepare to meet a conqueror.

Aurelia: O Catiline, meanest thou to destroy thy country? Is this the day appointed for destruction?

Catiline: To-day I purpose to chastise my foes; All is prepared.

Aurelia: Begin then with Aurelia; For I had rather perish by thy hand, Than live to share thy guilt.

Catiline: O let the tie That binds us—

Cethegus: Drive not thus to desperation A husband and a friend, who trusts his all To thee; thou art entered in the paths of glory, And to retreat were fatal.

Aurelia: Misery And sure destruction were Aurelia's fate: From that unhappy moment, when by thee And thy vile counsels led, I gave my hand To Catiline; despised, neglected, long Have I beheld, with eyes of detestation, Your horrid plots: spite of myself you made me A vile accomplice; but you know I loved, And basely have imposed upon my weakness: I blush to think how grossly you abused A woman's fond credulity; but know I'll no longer be guilty of a crime Which I abhor: no longer serve a tyrant: No, I renounce my vows, my faith to thee; These hands shall rise against thee, thou vile traitor: Henceforth I am thy foe. Strike, Catiline, strike; Destroy me; carry into burning Rome, For thy first victim, an expiring wife Slain by thy hand; destroy the hapless infant, Sad pledge of our detested nuptials: then, Barbarian as thou art, complete thy guilt, And in the blood of millions glut thy vengeance.

Catiline: And is the gentle, kind Aurelia then Amongst my foes? thus in the noblest war, That e'er was waged for freedom and for empire, When Pompey, Cæsar, Cato, are subdued, My worst of enemies at last are found In my own house; I am deserted there For an unworthy father: threatened too.

Aurelia: I threaten guilt, and tremble for—a husband: Even in my rage thou seest my tenderness; Abuse it not, it is my only weakness: But I would have thee fear—

Catiline: That word, Aurelia, Was never made for Catiline—but hear me: I love thee; yet presume not on thy power, Nor think I e'er will sacrifice my friends, My noble cause, my interest, and my fame, Glory and empire: no, it is enough If I forgive and pity thee, but know—

Aurelia: The crown thy pride looks up to I despise: I should behold it as the shameful mark Of infamy: thou showest thy love for me By pity and forgiveness; and I mine, By holding back, if possible, thy hand From guilt and error—therefore will I go—

SCENE III.

Catiline, Cethegus, Lentulus-Sura, Aurelia, etc.

Lentulus-Sura: We are discovered, lost, undone; our friends Betrayed, our plots unravelled all; Præneste Not yielded to us; Nonnius is in Rome; One of our spies is seized, and has confessed; Nonnius in open senate will accuse His son-in-law; he's gone to Cicero, Who knows too much already.

Aurelia: Now behold The fruits of guilt, and all thy great designs, Thy boasted fortunes, empire, and the throne, Which I despised: are thy eyes opened yet?

Catiline: [After a long pause.] This is a blow I thought not of; but say, Wilt thou betray me?

Aurelia: 'Tis what thou deservest: My country claims, and heaven demands it of me; But I'll do more, I'll save both Rome and thee; And though I have not all thy rage, may boast Some of thy courage; love will make me brave: Long since I saw thy danger, Catiline: 'Tis come, and now I will partake it with thee; I'll see my father, and obtain thy life, Or lose my own; I know he is forgiving, Gentle, and mild: I know he loves Aurelia, And will not urge too far a foe like thee, Desperate and brave; I'll talk to Cicero Who fears, and to the senate who adores thee; They will be glad to think thee innocent; Those whom we fear we readily forgive: But let sincerest penitence atone For thy past crimes: convicted guilt by that, And that alone, can hope for pardon; though I know it hurts thy pride, it must be done: At least I hope I shall procure thee time, Or to quit Rome, or to defend thyself: I'll not reproach thee; even when most guilty I loved, and in misfortune will not leave thee; But rather die to save thy life and glory. Farewell; let Catiline learn henceforth to trust me; I have deserved it.

Catiline: Sad alternative; It is most dreadful—but I yield to thee: Remember that a husband's plea is stronger, Much stronger than a father's: if I err, The crime is thine.

Aurelia: I'll take it all upon me; Nay, even thy hatred, if it must be so; I act for thee, and I'm satisfied. Daughter, and wife, and Roman, every duty Shall be performed; remember thine, and keep Thy heart as pure and spotless as Aurelia's.

SCENE IV.

Catiline, Cethegus, Lentulus-Sura, Freedmen.

lentulus-Sura: Is this the bold and fearless Catiline, Or Nonnius' timid son; a woman's slave; Appalled by phantoms? how thy great soul shrunk Soon as Aurelia spoke!

Cethegus: It cannot be; Catiline will never change; his noble soul By opposition grows but more resolved: Præneste lost, the senate our accusers, We may be conquerors still, and make them tremble Whilst they condemn us; we have noble friends, And will deserve them.

Lentulus-Sura: Ere the signal's given We may be seized; thou knowest at dead of night, Just as the senate part, we had agreed To execute our purpose: what, my friends, Must be resolved on?

Cethegus: [To Catiline.] Catiline, thou art silent, And tremblest too.

Catiline: I tremble at the blow Which I shall strike; my fate demands it of me.

Lentulus-Sura: I've no dependence on Aurelia: all That we can hope for is to sell our lives As dearly as we can.

Catiline: I count the moments, And weigh each circumstance; Aurelia's tears And flattery will a while suspend our fate; Cicero on other business is detained, And all is safe; let me have arms and men, No matter who they are, or slaves or free, Assassins, robbers, if they will but fight, We'll have them: thou brave Septimus, and thou My dearest Martian, whose approved zeal I shall depend on, must observe Aurelia; And Nonnius; when they're parted, talk to him About his daughter; tell him of her danger, Draw him by artful means to the dark path That leads to the Tiber, seize the lucky moment, And hurl him—ha! who's this?

SCENE V.

Cicero, Catiline, Cethegus, etc.

Cicero: Audacious traitor, Where art thou going? speak, Cethegus, who Assembled you?

Catiline: We'll tell thee in the senate.

Cethegus: There we shall see if thou art authorized Thus to pursue us.

Lentulus-Sura: Or what right The son of Tullius has to question us.

Cicero: At least I have a right to ask of these, Who brought them here: these are not like yourselves, Of senatorial rank; away with them. To prison.

Catiline: Darest thou thus on mere suspicion Confine a Roman; where's our liberty?

Cicero: They are of thy council, that's sufficient cause; Tremble, thyself; lictors, obey. [The lictors carry off Septimus and Martian.]

Catiline: 'Tis well: Go on, proud consul, and abuse thy power, The time will come when thou shalt answer for it.

Cicero: Instant I will examine them, hereafter Thus may I treat their masters; Nonnius knows All thy designs, Præneste's mine, and Rome Prepared for her defence; we soon shall see Which most prevails, or Catiline's artifice Or Cicero's vigilance: I do not preach Repentance and forgiveness to thee; no, I talk of punishment, thou mayest expect it: Come to the senate; follow if thou darest.

SCENE VI.

Catiline, Cethegus, Lentulus-Sura.

Cethegus: Must we at last then bend to Cicero, And own his hated power?

Catiline: To the last hour I will defy him: still his curious soul Pries into all, but can discover nothing: Our friends will only lead him more astray, By holding out false lights that will misguide His wandering footsteps: in that fatal scroll Cæsar's accused; the senate is divided, And Manlius with his army's at the gate: You think that all is lost, but follow me. And mark the event; we shall be conquerors still.

Lentulus-Sura: Nonnius, I fear, will make it all too plain.

Catiline: But he and Cicero shall never meet; Depend on that; away, address the senate With confidence, and leave the rest to me: But whither am I going?

Cethegus: Ha!

Catiline: Aurelia! O gods! what shall I do with that proud heart? Remove her from me: if I see my wife, Bold as I am, I shall relapse: away.

ACT IV.

SCENE I.

The Scene represents the place prepared for the reception of the Senate, with part of the gallery leading from Aurelia's palace to the temple of Tellus; a double row of benches in a circular form, with a raised seat for Cicero in the middle of it.

Cethegus, Lentulus-Sura.

Lentulus-Sura: These reverend fathers are exceeding slow, I thought ere this they would have met; perhaps Uncertain yet, and trembling for their fate, They know not how to act.

Cethegus: The oracle Of Rome, (for so he deems himself,) engaged In a continued round of toil, is busied In questioning his prisoner Septimus, Who will perplex him more; 'tis that retards Their meeting.

Lentulus-Sura: Would to heaven that we already Had taken up arms! I own I dread the senate. That reverence and attachment to the state, That sacred name of country, which awakes The sense of honor in each patriot breast; I like it not.

Cethegus: 'Tis nothing but a name, A word without a meaning; in the days Of our forefathers men respected it. Save a few stubborn stoics, none retain The memory of it; Cicero has raised Suspicions only; Cato's credit's lost; Cæsar is for us, what have we to fear? Defend yourselves, and Rome will be your own.

Lentulus-Sura: But what if Catiline, by an artful wife Seduced, at last should leave us; we have all Our weaknesses, and well thou knowest Aurelia Can lead him as she lists; he loves, esteems, And may be ruled by her.

Cethegus: His love will yield To his ambition.

Lentulus-Sura: Thou beheldest him tremble. In short, my friend, when tender ties like these—

Cethegus: [Taking him aside.] Cato approaches, let us listen to him. [Lentulus-Sura and Cethegus sit down at one corner of the Senate-house.]

SCENE II.

Catoenters the Senate Withlucullus, Crassus, Favonius, Clodius, Murena, Cæsar, Catullus, Marcellus, etc. **Cato**: [Observing the two conspirators.] Lucullus, mark those dangerous men; behold them In secret conference; see, the blush of guilt Glows on their cheeks at sight of me; already Treason with bold and shameless front stalks forth Amongst us, and the senate still dissemble Their knowledge of it; Sulla's demon sure Hath breathed its baneful influence o'er the souls Of our blind rulers.

Cethegus: Cato, thy rash censure May cost thee dear.

Cato: [Sits down, the other senators take their places.] The gods of Rome sometimes Permit a traitor's crimes to pass unpunished; They crushed our ancestors beneath the yoke Of cruel tyrants; shall imperial Rome, The mistress of the world, again submit To slavery? no: the guilt she spared in Sulla, In Catiline and Cethegus she may punish.

Cæsar: Cato, what meanest thou? thy outrageous virtue Can serve no purpose but to make thee foes.

Cato: [To Cæsar.] Cæsar is still the factious leader's friend, The patron of corruption, and preserves A soul unmoved whate'er his country suffers.

Cæsar: When danger calls, my country will not say I am too calm, therefore complain not, Cato.

Cato: I must complain, must weep the fate of Rome, Deserted and betrayed: now where is Pompey? Would he were here to save us!

Cæsar: Why not call On Cæsar?

Cato: Pompey loves his country

Cæsar: That Would I dispute with him.

SCENE III.

Cicero: [Entering with precipitation, the senators rise.] Why waste ye thus in idle altercation, The precious time when Rome is on the brink Of ruin, whilst on you she calls for succor, When the dread signal is already given? Already is this land of freedom stained With senatorial blood.

Lucullus: O heavens!

Cato: What sayest thou?

Cicero: The equestrian cohort, formed by my command, Were posted where they best might quell the foe; Nonnius, my friend, that generous old man, Who, amidst the crimes of this degenerate age, Still uncorrupted, from Præneste came, To guide us through this labyrinth of treason, And lead our wandering steps to peace and safety, When lo! two bloody ruffians rushed upon him, And plunged their daggers in his faithful heart: He fell: confusion followed, and wild uproar Amongst the people: we pursued the traitors, Spite of the multitude that thronged around them, And night's dark shade to favor their escape: One I have seized, and bound in chains; already He has confessed that Catiline set him on.

SCENE IV.

Catiline: [Standing up between Cato and Cæsar, Cethegus next to Cæsar, the Senate seated.] Yes, reverend fathers, know, the deed was mine; I slew your foes; 'twas Catiline who revenged His injured country, and destroyed a traitor.

Cicero: Barbarian, thou?

Cato: And darest thou boast of it?

Cæsar: Remember, fathers, we've no right to punish Before we hear him.

Cethegus: Speak, defend thyself, And triumph o'er the malice of thy foes.

Cicero: Romans, where are we?

Catiline: Amidst evil days And evil men, the horrors of foul discord And civil war; amidst determined foes, Whom I alone must conquer; Sulla's spirit Inspires once more the haughty sons of Rome: With grief I see expiring liberty, With grief behold this reverend senate torn By discord, horrors spread on every side, And Cicero pouring in the senate's ear Unjust suspicions: Cicero talks for Rome, But I avenge her: I have shown her cause Is dearer far to me than e'er it was To your proud consul. Nonnius was the soul, The leader of this foul conspiracy: It was a dangerous crisis; I stepped forth And saved you all: thus by a soldier fell The daring Spurius; thus was Gracchus slain By the brave Scipio: who shall punish me For acting like a Roman? which of you Will dare accuse me?

Cicero: I, who know thy crime; I, who can prove it—bring those freedmen here, Let them be heard. Fathers, behold the man Who has destroyed a senator of Rome: Will ye permit him thus to speak, to boast Of his foul deed, and call his crime a virtue?

Catiline: And will ye, Romans, let this vile accuser Thus persecute your fellow-citizens, Your best, your noblest friends? but know from me What Cicero could not tell you, and improve The important secret to your best advantage: In his own palace, know, this impious man, This vile betrayer, Nonnius, had concealed Arms, torches, all the instruments of death Designed for our destruction: if Rome lives, She lives by me, and to this arm you owe Your safety: send and seize them, and then say What's due to Catiline from his thankless country.

Cicero: [To the lictors.] Go you to the palace, bring with you the daughter Of Nonnius—ha! thou tremblest.

Catiline: I? 'tis false: Know, I despise this mean, this last resource Of disappointed malice—fathers, say, Have I not cleared myself? are you convinced!

Cicero: I am, that thou art guilty: can ye think That good old man was ever capable Of such detested fraud? it was thy art, Thy cunning, miscreant, to conceal from me Thy treachery; therefore didst thou choose the palace Of Nonnius to secrete thy instruments Of vengeance; there thou wouldst have hid thy guilt: Perhaps thou hast seduced his wretched daughter: Alas! his family is not the first Where thou hast carried sorrows, crimes, and death; And now thou wouldst destroy thy country too; Yet boldly darest, instead of punishment, To call for approbation and reward. O thou abandoned traitor, murderer, Reviler, hypocrite; such titles suit Thy boasted services. O you, who once Stood forth the happy patrons of mankind, The sovereign judges of the world, at length Will you submit, to let a tyrant hold Dominion o'er you, will you shut your eyes And rush into the precipice? awake, Revenge yourselves, or you partake his guilt: This day or Rome or Catiline must perish: Lose not a moment therefore, but determine:

Cæsar: Judgments too quickly made are oft unjust: This is the cause of Rome, and therefore merits Our strict attention: when our equals lag Beneath the stroke of censure, we should act With caution, and in them respect ourselves: Too much severity suits none but tyrants.

Cato: Too much indulgence here suits none but traitors. What! balance 'twixt a murderer and Rome! Is it not Cicero speaks, and shall we doubt?

Cæsar: These are suspicions only; give us proof: The arms once found, and Nonnius' guilt confirmed, Catiline deserves our praise. [Turning to Catiline.] Thou knowest I'll keep My word with thee in all things.

Cicero: O my country! O Rome! O gods! thus shall a hero plead A traitor's cause; art thou the senate's friend, And canst be Catiline's? henceforth Rome has naught To fear but from her own ungrateful sons.

Clodius: Rome is in safety; Cæsar loves his country, And we should think with him.

Cicero: It well becomes A man like Clodius to unite with those Who plan destruction, and delight in ruin: But whereso'er I turn my eyes, they meet With bold conspirators, or citizens Cold and inactive in the cause of Rome: Catiline, without or fear or danger, drives The storm upon us; he proscribes the senate; Already reaps in thought the bloody harvest; Marks out his victims, threatens, and commands; And when I point out the dread consequence, Then Cæsar talks of senatorial rights, And Clodius joins him: Cicero must be dumb: Catiline has murdered Nonnius; he who takes Another's life should lose his own; no rights, No laws should plead for him: the first great care Is to defend our country; but, alas! That country is no more.

SCENE V.

The Senate, Aurelia.

Aurelia: Ye great avengers Of innocence oppressed, my only hope, And thou, O consul, virtue's kind protector, To thee my murdered father calls for vengeance: O let me wash thy feet with tears—assist, [She falls at Cicero's feet; he raises her up.] Avenge me: tell me, if thou canst, who slew My father.

Cicero: There he stands. [Pointing to Catiline.]

Aurelia: O gods!

Cicero: 'Twas he Who did the deed, and boasts of it.

Aurelia: Good heaven! Can it be Catiline? did I hear aright? O bloody monster, didst thou murder him? [The Lictors support her.]

Catiline: [Turning to Cethegus, and fainting in his arms.] This is a dreadful sight—support me—this Is punishment enough.

Cethegus: Why droops my friend? Aurelia calls for vengeance: but if Catiline Has served his country, what has he to fear?

Catiline: [Turning to Aurelia.] Aurelia, 'tis too true—my cruel duty— My country—think me not so base; Aurelia Thou knowest my love, my tenderness—but ties Of a more sacred nature, ties—

SCENE VI.

The Senate, Aurelia, Chief of the Lictors.

Chief Lictor: My lord, We've seized these arms.

Cicero: At Nonnius's?

Chief Lictor: His house Was the receptacle of all: our prisoners Accuse him as the chief conspirator.

Aurelia: Malice and calumny! the lying slaves First take his life, and then destroy his fame: The wretch whose murderous hand—

Cicero: Go on—

Aurelia: Just gods. For what have ye reserved me?

Cicero: Speak: let truth In open day appear: but at the sight Of him you tremble; your dejected eyes, And sudden silence, show how much you dread The tyrant.

Aurelia: I have been to blame; Aurelia Alone is guilty.

Catiline: No; thou art not.

Aurelia: Hence, Detested monster, I abhor thy pity, Disclaim all converse, all relation with thee: Alas! too late, I see my guilt; too late Confess my crimes; yes, reverend fathers; yes, Aurelia knew the traitor, and concealed him: I asked for aid, but merit punishment; My weakness may be fatal; Rome's in danger; The world this day may be subverted: thou, Thou traitor, ledst me to the dark abyss Of infamy; thou madest my tenderness Subservient to thy wicked purposes; Curse on the guilty hour that gave my heart To Catiline; to thee I have been faithful, But false to heaven, and to my country; false To my unhappy father: I betrayed, And I destroyed him. [Whilst Aurelia is speaking, Cicero seems deeply affected.] Ye avenging gods, Ye sacred walls, and thou much injured spirit Of my dear father, Romans, senators, Behold my husband, your inveterate foe. [Turning to Catiline.] Now, miscreant, mark, and imitate Aurelia. [Stabs herself.]

Catiline: O wretched Catiline!

Cato: O dreadful day!

Cicero: [Rising.] 'Tis worthy of this guilty age.

Aurelia: O consul! There was a letter sent you—murder threatens On every side—take heed—alas!—I die. [Aurelia is carried off.]

Cicero: Let her have needful succor: Aufidus, Search for that paper—still are ye in doubt; Still will ye suffer this vile murderer To lord it o'er the senate, shall the deaths Of Nonnius and Aurelia pass unpunished?

Catiline: The guilt was thine: thy rancor and fell hatred Of Catiline urged him to the deed; ambition Inspired us both; thy happier fortune soared Above me, thou hast been the cause of all: I hate thee, Cicero, hate Rome itself For loving thee: long have I sought thy ruin, And I will seek it still: the wrongs I suffer Shall be revenged on thee; thy blood shall pay For mine; inconstant Rome, that now adores thee, Shall one day see with joy the mangled limbs Of her proud consul scattered o'er the senate: Remember Catiline has foretold thy fate; I hasten to accomplish it: farewell.

Cicero: Guards, seize the traitor.

Cethegus: Let them if they dare.

lentulus-Sura: The senate is divided: we defy thee.

Catiline: The war then is declared: friends, follow me, We must to battle: the uncertain senate Will think on't, and determine at their leisure. [He goes out with some senators of his party.]

Cicero: Now, ye illustrious conquerors of the world, Which will ye choose, or slavery or empire: Where is the freedom, where the majesty Of ancient Rome? where is her lustre now? 'Tis faded all: awake, my slumbering country; Lucullus, Cæsar, and Murena, listen; O listen to the voice of Rome; she calls Aloud for help, demands some gallant leader To fight for her; equality of rank Must be reserved for happier times, the Gauls Are here, Camillus must be found, we want A chief, a warrior, a dictator; now Name the most worthy, and I'll follow him.

SCENE VII.

The Senate, Chief Lictor.

Chief Lictor: My lord, I found this letter to Aurelia From Nonnius: all our cares for her were vain.

Cicero: [Reading the letter.] More dangers threatening! "Cæsar, who betrays us, Would seize Præneste," ha! [Turning to Cæsar.] Art thou too, Cæsar, A vile accomplice? this completes our woes; And wilt thou bend beneath a tyrant?—read it.

Cæsar: I have: I am a Roman, ruin comes Upon us, danger is on every side; 'Tis well: I must be gone: you have my answer.

Cato: It was a doubtful one: most certainly He is their friend.

Cicero: Away: let us defend The state against them all: O Senators! If Nonnius' death, if poor Aurelia's pangs, If bleeding Rome, if a subverted world Have power to stir up your resentment, rise, Fly to the capitol, defend your gods, Defend your country, punish Catiline. I'll not reproach you; though 'twas most unkind, To spurn at Cicero, and embrace a villain. But to avoid a tyrant, name your chief: You, who are friends to virtue, separate From traitors. [The Senators separate themselves from Cethegus and Lentulus-Sura.] Now let us unite, my friends, Never let quarrels, jealousies, and strife, Divide us; 'twas by them that Sulla triumphed. For me, wherever danger calls, I go Intrepid and inflexible: O gods! Strengthen this arm, and animate this voice: O grant me still to save ungrateful Rome!

ACT V.

SCENE I.

Cato, with Part of the Senate in Arms.

Clodius: [To Cato.] What! whilst the senate armed for its own safety From busy faction's power can scarce preserve These sacred walls; thus shall a proud plebeian Insult us? shall a people, born to freedom, Be treated like dependent slaves? by him, Shall Rome's best friends, the conquerors of the world, Be put in chains? because he is a consul, Shall he condemn his masters? Catiline's self Were less despotic, and less dangerous: With you I feel my country's wretchedness, And weep her fate; but cannot, will not, see The senate thus disgraced.

Cato: Disgrace attends On those alone who merit it—but know, The blood of nobles, your patrician friends, Debased by guilt, should rank below the meanest; Those who betrayed us are condemned to death: Cicero condemned them; he who saved your country, The glorious consul, whom ye dare accuse, Because he loved you but too well: yet fear And tremble all, ungrateful as ye are To join with traitors, for an equal fate Shall soon o'erwhelm you; Catiline's at our gates. What Cæsar hath determined yet we know not; Whether he means to save, or to destroy His country: Cicero bravely acts alone, And hazards all for Rome, whilst you despise Your best of friends, and treat him as a foe.

Clodius: Cato has more severity than courage, And ever rigorous, hates not guilt so much As he loves punishment: reproach us not, Nor act the censor when we want a friend. Whilst the destructive flames of war surround, 'Tis not a consul's edict can defend us. What can your lictor and his fasces do, Against a band of fierce conspirators? You talk of dangers, and of Cæsar's power: Who does not know that Cæsar is the friend Of Catiline? you have pointed out the ills That threaten Rome; it were a nobler task To show us how we may remove them.

Cato: Yes; And so I will: I would advise the senate To be aware of Cæsar, and of—thee; Nay, more—but see our father comes.

SCENE II.

Cicero, Cato, Part of the Senate.

Cato: [To Cicero.] Behold Great Cicero, the sons of thankless Rome: Approach and save us; envy's self shall soon Fall at thy feet, in humble admiration Of such transcendent virtue.

Cicero: Friends and Romans, The love of glory is my ruling passion, Fame is the fair reward of human toil, And I would wish to merit it from you: I have done little yet, perhaps hereafter I may do more to serve my country: Rome Was full of open and of secret foes; Patricians, and plebeians, citizens And soldiers, all in wild confusion, seemed To thirst for blood: I saw the gathering storm That threatened universal ruin; saw The bold conspirators tumultuous rise, And bear down all before them: at their head Were Sura and Cethegus; them I seized, And gave to justice; but the Hydra faction Hath many heads which still successive rise, And mock my labors: Catiline boldly pushed To the Quirinal gate; by gallant deeds, Almost incredible, he kept the field, And forced a passage to his army; Rome Beheld him with amazement; Antony In vain opposing Sulla's hardy veterans, Was baffled and subdued; Petreius strove To succor him, but with unequal force And fruitless valor: thus on every side, Surrounded by calamities, great Rome, The mistress of the world, is on the brink Of ruin; Cicero trembles for her fate.

Crassus: What part hath Cæsar taken?

Cicero: He hath behaved As Cæsar must, with most undaunted courage, Yet not as Rome could wish a zealous friend Would act in her defence. I saw him quell The rebel foe; yet after that, stir up Seditious spirits, and by every art Of smooth insinuation, work himself Into the people's hearts. Amidst this scene Of blood, methought a secret joy o'erspread His glowing cheek, whilst his all-soothing voice Courted applause, inviting Rome to be His slave hereafter.

Cato: I was ever fearful Of Cæsar's power; he is not to be trusted.

SCENE III.

The Senate, Cæsar.

Cæsar: Well: am I still suspected in the senate? Is Cato's stubborn virtue still my foe? Of what does he accuse me?

Cato: As a friend To Catiline, the sworn enemy of Rome; You have protected him, and leagued with those It had become you better to chastise.

Cæsar: I would not stain my laurels with the blood Of such vile miscreants: Cæsar fights with none But warriors.

Cato: What are these conspirators?

Cæsar: A dastard crowd, contemptible and vile: They fled like slaves before me; but the soldiers Of Sulla are a formidable band, And boast an able chief; from them indeed Rome hath some cause to fear; Petreius sinks Beneath his wounds, and Catiline marches onward; Our soldiers are alarmed: what says our consul? And what has he resolved?

Cicero: I'll tell thee, Cæsar: Grant, heaven, we may succeed!—thou hast deserved Suspicion, but I'll give thee the fair means To clear thy honor, and avenge thy country. I know thee well, thy virtues and thy frailty; Know what thou canst, and what thou darest not do; Know Cæsar would command, but not betray, A noble friend, and a most dangerous foe: Whilst I condemn I cannot but esteem thee. Away: remember that the eyes of Rome, And of the world, are on thee: go, support Petreius, save the empire, and deserve The love of Cato: we have men, but want A general to conduct them; Cæsar best Can lead them, and to him alone we trust The safety and the glory of mankind.

Cæsar: Cicero on Cæsar safely may depend; Farewell: I go to conquer or to die. [Exit.]

Cato: You've touched him in the tenderest part; ambition Will urge him on.

Cicero: Great souls must ever thus Be treated: I have bound him to the state By this firm confidence; I know his valor Will now support us: the ambitious still Should be distinguished from the traitor; I Shall make him virtuous if he is not so Already. Courage, as directed, forms The mighty hero, or the mighty villain; And he who is renowned for guilt alone, Had glory fired his breast, to him had been The incense poured, to him the temple raised For his exalted merit: Catiline's self, By me conducted, had like Scipio shone: Though many a Sulla is in Cæsar hid, Yet doubt I not but Rome shall find in him Her best support. [Turning to the chief of the Lictors, who enters armed.] Well: these conspirators, What have they done?

Chief Lictor: My lord, they met the fate They merited, but other foes rise up, Sprung from their blood; like Ætna's flames, that burst From the parched entrails of the burning mount: Another Hannibal, but far more dreadful, Because amongst the guilty sons of Rome He finds his traitorous friends, is at our gates. A hundred voices roar for Catiline, Condemn your laws, and curse your tardy senate; Demand their ancient rights, and cry aloud For vengeance on the consul.

Clodius: Well indeed They may, while Cicero tramples on the laws, And spurns his equals thus; perhaps the senate—

Cicero: Clodius, no more; restrain thy envious tongue, Nor rashly blame the guiltless; my short power Will soon be wrested from me; whilst it lasts It shall not be controlled; you will have time Enough to vex and persecute hereafter; But whilst the state's in danger, Cicero claims The tribute of respect: I know too well This fickle world to hope for constancy And candor from it; foul ingratitude Is all that I expect; on false surmises Great Scipio was accused; he thanked the gods, And quitted Rome: I too will pay my vows To gracious heaven, but will not leave you; no; My days are all devoted to my country, And all shall be expended in her service.

Cato: Suppose I were to show myself in Rome, Perhaps my presence might disperse the crowd, And be a check on Cæsar, whom I own I much suspect: if fortune frowns upon us—

Cicero: We cannot do without you in the senate; I've given my orders; Cæsar's in the field; Thy great example may be useful here, And Rome's expiring glory be restored By Cato's virtue—but behold he comes, And crowned with victory. [Cæsar enters; Cicero embraces him.] Most noble Cæsar, Hast thou preserved the state?—

Cæsar: I hope so: now The consul will believe me—brave Petreius Has gained immortal glory: here we fought, Beneath this sacred rampart, in the sight Of our domestic gods that fired each soul With nobler rage: Metellus, and Murena, With the brave Scipios showed in Rome's defence The same exalted courage that subdued Asia and Carthage; they have merited Most nobly of their country: touching Cæsar Let others speak: the desperate remains Of Sulla's army seemed to brave their fate, And in the agonies of death breathed forth Their curses on us: midst the general slaughter, The fiery Catiline long undaunted stood, Fought through a host of circling foes, till spent With ceaseless toil, and covered o'er with wounds, Bravely he fell: I must admire the soldier, Though I detest the rebel: once I loved him, I own it; but let Cicero judge, if ever To friendship Cæsar sacrificed his honor.

Cicero: Cæsar is all that Cicero could desire, All that he wished, and all he hoped to find him: Go on, brave youth, preserve thy noble spirit, And be thy country's friend; may heaven protect And guard thee: never may thy generous soul Be stained with vice, nor false ambition urge Thy spotless youth to quit the paths of virtue!

End

www.ingramcontent.com/pod-product-compliance
Lightning Source LLC
Chambersburg PA
CBHW031439040426
42444CB00006B/880